Doreen Smith

Violin Sight-Reading

Book 1

Music Department
OXFORD UNIVERSITY PRESS
Oxford and New York

NOTE

These graded sight-reading pieces for the violin are designed to provide practice material at all stages. Book 1 begins with the first position and covers the usual examination expectations for the earlier grades. More advanced players will find exercises requiring use of the higher registers, and the need for more technical expertise in book 2.

Fingering and bowing

There are as many fingerings and bowings as there are players. Those marked here are simply one way of performing a piece; they are by no means obligatory. The aim is to give as musical an impression as possible after a brief study of the piece, and to enjoy exploring the instrument.

To the violinist — what to do before you play

Look at:

- The **foreign words** which will suggest the speed, mood, and style.
- The **key signature**: work out your finger patterns on each string.
- The **time signature**: are you going to count in beats, or would it be more helpful to sub-divide each beat?
- **Changes** of key signature or time signature (in higher grades).
- **Unusual** time patterns, accidentals, rests, staccato notes, slurs, and dynamics.
- The **speed**: decide on the speed and count at least one bar before you begin. Count aloud throughout.

Keep going, and try to give an overall impression of the music.

Doreen Smith, 1992

VIOLIN SIGHT-READING, BOOK 1

by DOREEN SMITH

GRADE 1

© Oxford University Press 1992

Printed in Great Britain

OXFORD UNIVERSITY PRESS, MUSIC DEPARTMENT, GREAT CLARENDON STREET, OXFORD OX2 6DP

Photocopying this copyright material is ILLEGAL.

4

Dance

7

mp

mf　　　　　　　　　　　　　　*dim.*

Marked

8

f

Waltz

9

mf cantabile

Brightly

10

mp　　　　　　*f*

mp　　　　　　*f*

Slowly and with a singing tone

11

mf

Andante

12

mp　　　　　　　　　　　　　　*cresc.*

dim. e rit.

6

Andante

19

Andante

20

GRADE 2

Hornpipe

1

Lively

2

Sadly

3

Moderato

Andante

Allegretto

Adagio

Adagio

Allegro

Adagio

20

GRADE 3

At a steady pace

1

Andante

2

Adagio

3

Vivo

Allegro

Vivace

Allegretto

Lento

Andantine

9

Allegro

10

Allegro

11

a tempo

Allegretto grazioso

12

Adagio

18

mp molto legato e cantabile

p   *cresc.*

Sadly

19

mp dolce

Allegretto

20

mf

rit.

GRADE 4

Moderato

1

mf

Adagio

Allegretto

Andante cantabile

Vivace

Scherzando

16

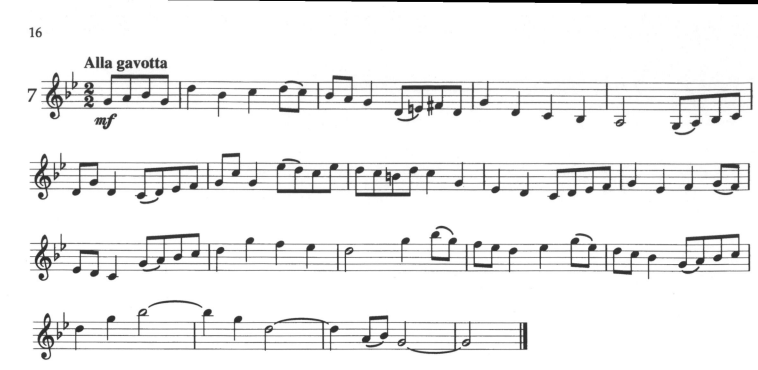

Alla gavotta

Alla marcia

Allegro vivace

Allegretto

Andante

11

mp molto legato

cresc.

dim. e poco rit.

Grandioso

12

mf

poco rit.

Sarabande

13

mp *cresc.* *mf*

p *cresc.* *dim. e poco rit.*

Allegro vivace

14

mf

mp dolce

cresc.

Adagio (second position throughout)

Andante cantabile

Andantino

Moderato

Vivace

19

Andante tranquillo

20

GRADE 5

Allegretto

1

Moderato

2

20

Presto

7

Andante

8

Allegro moderato

9

Allegro vivace

10

Waltz

11

Printed in England by Caligraving Limited Thetford Norfolk